DISCOGRAPHY

BUFFALO SPRINGFIELD (ATCO RECORDS)

BUFFALO SPRINGFIELD	FEBRUARY 1967
BUFFALO SPRINGFIELD AGAIN	DECEMBER 1967
LAST TIME AROUND	AUGUST 1968
THE BEST OF THE BUFFALO SPRINGFIELD/ RETROSPECTIVE	JANUARY 1969

NEIL YOUNG (REPRISE RECORDS)

NEIL YOUNG	JANUARY 1969
EVERYBODY KNOWS THIS IS NO WHERE	MAY 1969

CONTENTS

SUGAR MOUNTAIN

Oh, to live on Sugar Mountain
With the barkers and the colored balloons,
You can't be twenty on Sugar Mountain,
Tho' you're thinkin' that you're leavin' there too soon,
You're leavin' there too soon.

It's so noisy at the fair but all your friends are there
And the candy floss you had and your mother and your dad.

Oh, to live on Sugar Mountain
With the barkers and the colored balloons,
You can't be twenty on Sugar Mountain,
Tho' you're thinkin' that you're leavin' there too soon,

Now you're underneath the stairs and you're givin' back some glares
To the people that you met and it's your first cigarette.

Oh, to live on Sugar Mountain
With the barkers and the colored balloons,
You can't be twenty on Sugar Mountain,
Tho' you're thinkin' that you're leavin' there too soon,
You're leavin' there too soon.

There's a girl just down the aisle,
Oh, to turn and see her smile.
You can hear the words she wrote as you read the hidden note.

Chorus

Now you say you're leavin' home
'Cause you want to be alone.
Ain't it funny how you feel when you're findin' out it's real?

Chorus

BY NEIL YOUNG © 1968 COTILLION MUSIC, INC. & BROKEN FIDDLE
All rights administered by WARNER-TAMERLANE PUBLISHING CORP.
All Rights Reserved

SUGAR MOUNTAIN

Words and Music by
NEIL YOUNG

Moderately

* Guitar

Keyboard

Oh,__ to live on__ Sug - ar Moun - tain __

with the bark - ers and the col - ored__ bal - loons, __

You can't__ be twen - ty on Sug - ar Moun - tain,

* Guitarists: Tune all strings down one whole step to a D-based tuning.

Dm / Cm

tho' you're think-in' that you're leav - in' there_ too_____ soon,_

Dm / Cm **G / F**

you're leav-in' there_____ too_____ soon._

G / F **F(addG) / Eb(addF)**

It's so nois-y at_ the fair___ but all your friends are_

There's a girl_ just down the aisle,_ oh, to turn and see her_

there_ And the can - dy floss you had ____ and your moth-
smile._ You can hear the words_ she wrote ____ as you read_

er and your dad._
the hid - den note._ Oh,_ to live on_

Sug - ar Moun - tain_ with the bark - ers and the col-

ored_ bal - loons,_ You can't_ be twen - ty

on Sug-ar Moun - tain, tho' you're think-in' that you're leav-

in' there_ too _____ soon, _ you're leav - in' there_

_____ too _____ soon. _

Now you're un-der-neath the stairs __ and you're giv-in' back __ some glares __
Now you say you're leav - in' home __ 'cause you want __ to be a-lone. __

__ To the peo-ple who you met __ and it's your __
__ Ain't it fun-ny how you feel __ when you're find -

first __ cig - a - rette.
in' out __ it's real?

Oh, to live __ on __ Sug - ar Moun - tain __

with the bark - ers and the col - ored ___ bal - loons, ___

You can't ___ be twen - ty on Sug - ar Moun - tain,

To Coda ⊕

tho' you're think - in' that you're leav - in' there ___ too _____ soon, ___

you're leav - in' there _____ too _____ soon. ___

Coda

tho' you're think-in' that you're leav - in' there____ too____ soon.____

NOWADAYS CLANCY CAN'T EVEN SING

Hey, who's that stompin' all over my face,
Where's that silhouette I'm tryin' to trace,
Who's puttin' sponge in the bells I once rung
And takin' my gypsy before she's begun
To singin', the meaning of what's in my mind,
Before I can take home what's rightfully mine.
Joinin' and list'nin' and talkin' in rhymes,
Stoppin' the feelin' to wait for the time.

And who's sayin', "Baby, that don't mean a thing
'Cause now a-days Clancy can't even sing"?

And who's all hung up on that happiness thing,
Who's tryin' to tune all the bells that he rings,
And who's in the corner and down on the floor
With pencil and paper, just countin' the score?
Who's tryin' to act like he's just in between?
The night isn't black if you know that it's green.
But don't bother lookin', you're too blind to see
Who's comin' on like he wanted to be.

And who's sayin', "Baby, that don't mean a thing
'Cause now a-days Clancy can't even sing"?

And who's comin' home on old ninety five,
Who's got the feelin' to keep him alive?
Though havin' it, sharin' it ain't quite the same,
It ain't a gold nugget, you can't lay a claim.
Who's seein' eyes through the crack in the floor?
There it is, baby, don't you worry no more.
Who should be sleeping, but's writin' this song,
Wishin' and hopin' he weren't so damn wrong?

And who's sayin', "Baby, that don't mean a thing
'Cause now a-days Clancy can't even sing"?

NOWADAYS CLANCY CAN'T EVEN SING

17

Words and Music by
NEIL YOUNG

1. Hey, who's that stomp-in' all o-ver my face,_ Where's that sil-hou-ette_ I'm_ try-in' to trace,_ Who's put-tin' sponge_ in the bells_ I once rung_ And tak-in' my gyp-sy be-fore_____ she's be-gun?_____ To

© 1966, 1974 COTILLION MUSIC, INC., TEN EAST MUSIC, SPRINGALO TOONES and RICHIE FURAY MUSIC
All rights administered by WARNER-TAMERLANE PUBLISHING CORP.
All Rights Reserved

sing - in'_ the mean-ing of_ what's in my_ mind, be - fore I can take home what's

right-ful-ly mine. Join - in' and a -list -'nin' and_ talk - in' in rhymes,

stop -pin' the feel - in' to wait for the time.

Who's say-in', "Ba -by, that don't_ mean a thing_ 'cause now -a-days Clan - cy

(Verse 1, continued) can't ... e-ven sing?"

2. And who's all hung up on that hap-pi-ness thing,__ Who's try-in' to tune all the bells that he rings,__ And who's in the cor-ner and down on the floor__ With pen-cil and pa-per, just count-in' the score?__

(Vocal harmony)
Am Dm Am
Bm Em Bm
Who's try-in' to act like he's just in be-tween? The night is-n't black_ if you know_
Dm Am Dm
Em Bm Em
__ that it's green._ But don't both - er look-ing, you're_ too blind to see
Am Dm F
Bm Em G
who's com-in' on like he want-ed to be. Who's say-in', "Ba-by, that don't_
R. H.
G Am C Dm Dm7 Em Am
A Bm D Em Em7 F♯m Bm
__ mean a thing__ 'cause now-a-days Clan-cy can't e-ven sing?"

Cmaj7 Fmaj7 Cmaj7 Fmaj7
Dmaj7 Gmaj7 Dmaj7 (Solo) Gmaj7

3. And who's com-in' home on old ___ nine-ty-five, ___

Cmaj7 Fmaj7 Cmaj7
Dmaj7 Gmaj7 Dmaj7

Who's got the feel-in', yeah, to keep 'em a-live? Though hav-in' it, ___ shar-in' it ___

Fmaj7 Cmaj7 Fmaj7
Gmaj7 Dmaj7 Gmaj7

ain't quite the same, ___ It ain't a gold nug-get, you can't lay a claim. ___

Am Dm Am
Bm (Vocal harmony) Em Bm

Who's see-in' eyes through the crack in the floor? ___ There it is, Ba — by, don't you wor-ry no__ more. Who should be sleep-ing, but's a - writ- in' this__ song,

wish- in' and a-hop-in' he weren't so__ damn wrong? Who's say-in',"Ba-by,that don't__

__ mean a thing__'cause now-a-days Clan -cy can't e -ven sing?"

can't e - ven sing?"

BURNED

Been burned and with both feet on the ground,
I've learned that it's painful comin' down.
No use runnin' away, and there's no time left to stay;
Now I'm finding out that it's so confusin',
No time left and I know I'm losin'.

Flashed, and I think I'm fallin' down,
Crashed, and my ears can't hear a sound.
No use runnin' away, and there's no time left to stay;
Now I'm findin' out that it's so confusin',
No time left and I know I'm losin'.

Burned and with both feet on the ground,
I've learned that it's painful comin' down.
No use runnin' away, and there's no time left to stay;
Now I'm finding out that it's so confusin',
No time left and I know I'm losin'.

BURNED

Words and Music by
NEIL YOUNG

Moderately

1. Been burned and with
3. Burned and with

both feet on the ground, __
both feet on the ground, __

I've

learned that it's pain - ful com-in' down. __

No use run-nin' a-way, ___ and there's no time left to stay; ___

Now I'm find-ing out that it's so ___ con-fus-in', no ___ time ___ left and I know ___

_ I'm los-in'. 2. Flashed, and I think ___ I'm fall-in' down, ___
(Flashed, ___ and I think ___

Crashed, and my ears ___ can't hear a sound. ___
_ I'm fall-ing down. ___) (The sound. ___

No use run-nin' a-way, and there's no time left to stay;

Now I'm find-in' out that it's so con-fus-in',

no time left and I know I'm los-in'.

I'm los-in'.

DO I HAVE TO COME RIGHT OUT AND SAY IT?

Do I have to come right out and say it,
Tell you that you look so fine?
Do I have to come right out and ask you to be mine?
If it was a game, I could play it.
Tryin' to make it but I'm losin' time,
I gotta bring you in, you're over workin' my mind.

Indecision is crowding me,
I have no room to spare
And I can't believe she'd care.
Like a dream, she has taken me and now I don't know where,
And a part of me is scared,
The part of me I shared once before.

Do I have to come right out and say it,
Tell you that you look so fine?
Do I have to come right out and ask you to be mine?

If it was a game, I could play it.
Tryin' to make it but I'm losin' time,
I gotta bring you in, you're over workin' my mind.
Do I have to come right out and say it,
Tell you that you look so fine?

DO I HAVE TO COME RIGHT OUT AND SAY IT?

Words and Music by
NEIL YOUNG

Moderately

Do I have to come right out and say it, Tell you that you look so fine? Do I have to come right out and ask you to be mine? If it was a game, I could play it. Try-in' to make it but I'm losin' time,

part of me___ is scared,___ the part of me___ I

shared once be-fore._____ Do I have to come

Do I have to come

right out and say it,
right out and say it, girl,   Tell you that you look so fine?_   Do I have to come

right_ out and ask you to be mine?_____

Coda

G Tacet | **F** | **C**

— If it was — a game, I could play — it. Try-in' to make it but I'm—

F | **C** | **F** **C**

— los - in' time, I got - ta bring you in,— you're o -ver-work-in' my—

Dm7 | **G** Tacet | **F**

mind. Do I have to come right out and say it, girl,—

C | **F** | **C**

Tell you that you look so fine?—

OUT OF MY MIND

Out of my mind and I just can't take it anymore.
Left behind, by myself and what I'm living for.
All I hear are screams from outside the limousines
That are taking me out of my mind.

Out of my mind thru the key hole in an open door.
Happy to find that I don't know what I'm smiling for.
Tired of hanging on, if you miss me
I've just gone, 'cause they're taking me out of my mind.

Out of my mind and I just can't take it anymore.
Left behind, by myself and what I'm living for.
All I hear are screams from outside the limousines
That are taking me out of my mind.

OUT OF MY MIND

Words and Music by
NEIL YOUNG

Out of my _____ mind _____ and I _____ just can't _____ take it
out of my _____ mind _____ thru the _____ key - hole _____ in an
out of my _____ mind _____ and I _____ just can't _____ take it

E   A   E   D

an - y - more.___ / o - pen door.___ / an - y - more.___
Left be - hind / Hap - py to find / Left be - hind
by my - self and_ what I'm / that I ___ don't know_ what I'm / by my - self and_ what I'm

E   D   Bm

liv - ing for. / smil - ing for. / liv - ing for.
All I ___ hear are ___ screams ___ from out - / Tired of ___ hang - ing ___ on, _____ if you_ / All I ___ hear are ___ screams ___ from out -

Amaj7   F#m   D

side ___ the_ lim - ou - sines / ___ miss ___ me_ I've just gone, / side ___ the_ lim - ou - sines
that are ___ tak - ing me ___ / 'cause they're ___ tak - ing me ___ / that are ___ tak - ing me ___

1. 2.   3.
E(no3rd)   E(no3rd)   A   E

out of my ___ mind.___

FLYING ON THE GROUND IS WRONG

Is my world not fallin' down?
I'm in pieces on the ground
And my eyes aren't open
And I'm standin' on my knees.

But if crying and holding on
and flying on the ground is wrong,
Then I'm sorry to let you down,
But you're from my side of town, and I'll miss you.

Turn me up or turn me down,
Turn me off or turn me 'round.
I wish I could have met you in a place where we both belong.

But if crying and holding on
And flying on the ground is wrong,
Then I'm sorry to let you down,
But you're from my side of town, and I'll miss you.

Sometimes I feel like I'm just a helpless child,
Sometimes I feel like a king.
But baby, since I have changed,
I can't take nothin' home.

City lights at a country fair
Never shine, but always glare,
If I'm bright enough to see you,
You're just too dark to care.

But if crying and holding on
And flying on the ground is wrong,
Then I'm sorry to let you down,
But you're from my side of town, and I'll miss you.

FLYING ON THE GROUND IS WRONG

Words and Music by
NEIL YOUNG

1. Is my world not fall-en down? I'm in piec-es on the ground and my
(on the ground)

eyes aren't o-pen and I'm stand-in' on my knees. But if

E
(Vocal harmony)
Bm
D
cry - ing and hold - ing on and fly - ing on the ground is wrong,
(hold - ing on and fly - ing on the ground is wrong,
Bm
A
A+
D
To Coda
then I'm sor - ry to let you down, but you're from
then I'm sor - ry to let you down, but you're from
(optional)
Bm
A
Bm(addE)/A
Amaj7
5 fr.
Bm(addE)/A
my side of town, and I'll miss you.
my side of town, and I'll miss you.)
Am
Am7
Am6
Am
A
Bm(addE)/A
(Vocal harmony)
Amaj7
5 fr.
Bm(addE)/A
2. Turn me up or turn me down,
(turn me down,)

A
Bm(addE)/A
Amaj7
5 fr. (Vocal harmony)
Bm(addE)/A
A
Bm
turn me off or turn me 'round._ I wish I could have met you in a
(turn me 'round._ Ooh.
A
Bm(addE)/A
Amaj7
5 fr.
Bm(addE)/A
A
D.S. 𝄋 al Coda
place where we both_ be - long.
)
But if
Coda
Bm
A
Dm7
(Solo)
my side of town, and I'll miss you.
my side of town, and I'll_ miss you.)
Some - times I
G7
Em7
Am7
Dm7
feel like I'm just a help - less_ child,_
Some - times I
R.H.

G G7 C E Amaj7
5 fr.
feel like a king. But Ba - by, since I have
Bm(addE)/A Amaj7 Bm(addE)/A Amaj7
changed, I can't take nothin' home.
(home.
D A Bm(addE)/A Amaj7 Bm(addE)/A
(Solo)
(Vocal harmony)
3. Cit - y lights at a coun - try fair
(coun - try fair)
(Percussion)
A Bm(addE)/A Amaj7 Bm(addE)/A A Bm
nev - er shine, but al - ways glare, If I'm bright e - nough to see you,
(al - ways glare, ooh.

you're just too dark __ to __ care. __ But if

cry - ing and hold - ing __ on _____ and fly - ing on the ground is wrong, __
(hold - ing __ on _____ and fly - ing on the ground is wrong, __

___ then I'm sor - ry __ to let you down, __ but
___ then I'm sor - ry to let you down, __ but

you're from my side of town, and I'll miss you.
you're from my side of town, and I'll __ miss you.)

BROKEN ARROW

The lights turned on and the curtain fell down,
And when it was over it felt like a dream,
They stood at the stage door and begged for a scream,
The agents had paid for the black limousine that waited outside in the rain.

Did you see them,
Did you see them?
Did you see them in the river?
They were there to wave to you.
Could you tell that the empty quivered, brown skinned Indian
On the banks that were crowded and narrow,
Held a broken arrow?

Eighteen years of American dream,
He saw that his brother had sworn on the wall.
He hung up his eye lids and ran down the hall,
His mother had told him a trip was a fall,
And don't mention babies at all.

Did you see him,
Did you see him?
Did you see him in the river?
He was there to wave to you.
Could you tell that the empty quivered, brown skinned Indian
On the banks that were crowded and narrow,
Held a broken arrow?

The streets were lined for the wedding parade,
The Queen wore the white of the county of song,
The black covered caisson her horses had drawn
Protected her King from the sun rays of dawn.
They married for peace and were gone.

Did you see them
Did you see them
Did you see them in the river?
They were there to wave to you.
Could you tell that the empty quivered, brown skinned Indian
On the banks that were crowded and narrow,
Held a broken arrow?

BROKEN ARROW

Words and Music by
NEIL YOUNG

Moderately slow

1. The lights turned on and the cur-tain fell down, And when it was o-ver it felt like a dream, They stood at the stage-door and begged for a scream, The

a-gents had paid for the black lim-ou-sine that wait-ed out-side in the rain. Did you see them, did you see them? Did you see them in the riv-er? They were there to wave to you.

56

Could you tell that the emp-ty quiv-ered, brown - skinned In - di -

an on the banks that were crowd - ed and nar - row,

held a bro-ken ar - row?

3. The

2. Eight - een years of A - mer - i - can dream, He
   streets were lined for the wed - ding pa - rade, The

saw that his broth - er had sworn on the wall.___ He
Queen wore the white gloves, the coun - ty of song,___ The

hung up his eye - lids and ran down the hall,___ His
black cov - ered cais - son her hors - es had drawn pro -

moth - er had told ___ him a trip was a fall,___ And
tect - ed her King ___ from the sun rays of dawn.___ They

don't men - tion ba - bies at all. Did you see ___ him, ___ did you___
mar - ried for peace ___ and were gone. Did you see ___ them, ___ did you___

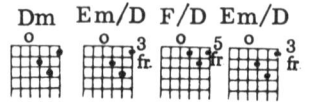

see him?
see them?

Did you see him in the riv-er?__ He was there to wave to you.__
Did you see them in the riv-er?__ They were there to wave to you.__

Could you tell that the emp-ty quiv-ered, brown - skinned In - di -

an on the banks that were crowd - ed and nar-row, held a ___ bro-ken ar - row?__

Fine

EXPECTING TO FLY

There you stood on the edge of your feather,
Expecting to fly.
While I laughed, I wondered whether I could wave goodbye,
Knowin' that you'd gone.
By the summer it was healing, we had said goodbye.
All the years we'd spent with feeling ended with a cry,
Babe, ended with a cry, Babe, ended with a cry.

I tried so hard to stand as I stumbled and fell to the ground
So hard to laugh as I fumbled and reached for the love I found,
Knowin' it was gone.
If I ever lived without you, now you know I died
If I ever said I loved you, now you know I tried Babe,
Now you know I tried Babe
Now you know I tried Babe

EXPECTING TO FLY

Words and Music by
NEIL YOUNG

Slowly

Guitar (Capo up 3 frets)
Keyboard

(Vocal harmony)

1. There you stood on the edge of your feath-er,

ex-pect-ing to fly. While I laughed, I won-dered wheth-er

I could wave good - bye, Know - in' that you'd

By the sum-mer__ it was heal-ing,
we had__ said good-bye.__ All__ the years we'd spent with feel-ing
end-ed with a cry,_____ Babe, end-ed with a cry,
Babe,_____ end-ed with a cry._____

gone.

2. I tried_ so hard_ to stand_ as I stum-bled and fell_ to the ground._

So hard_ to laugh_ as I fum-bled and reached for_ the love_ I

found,_____ know-in'_ it was gone._____

If I ev-er_ lived with-out you, now you_ know I'd die._

If I__ ev-er__ said__ I loved you, now__ you know I'd try,___

Babe, now you know I'd try. Babe,

now you know I'd try, Babe.___

Very slow four
Tacet

(opt.) *(opt.)* *rit.* *pp<mf>pp*

MR. SOUL

Oh, hello, Mister Soul, I dropped by to pick up a reason
For the thought that I caught that my head is the event of the season
Why in crowds just a trace of my face could seem so pleasin',
I'll cop out to the change, but a stranger is putting the tease on.

I was down on a frown when the messenger brought me a letter.
I was raised by the praise of a fan who said I upset her.
Any girl in the world could have easily known me better.
She said, "You're strange, but don't change;" and I let her.

In a while, will the smile on my face turn to plaster,
Stick around while the clown who is sick does the trick of disaster.
For the race of my head and my face is moving much faster.
Is it strange I should change? I don't know, why don't you ask her?

MR. SOUL

Moderate hard Rock

Words and Music by
NEIL YOUNG

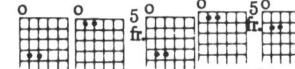

1. Oh, hel-lo,___ Mis-ter Soul,_ I dropped_ by to pick up a rea-

son For the thought__ that I caught__that my head__

___ is the e-vent of the sea-son. Why in crowds__

just a trace of my face could seem so pleas-in',

I'll cop out to the change, but a stran-ger is put-ting the tease on.

2. I was down on a frown when the mes-sen-ger brought me a let-ter.

(Vocal harmony) (brought me a let-ter.)

(Solo)

F#/E G/E 5fr. F#/E G/E 5fr. E5
F#/E G/E
(Vocal harmony) F#/E G/E
(who said I up -set ___

I was raised ___ by the praise of a fan who said I up -set ___

E5
___ her.)
F#/E G/E 5fr.
A5
F#/E G/E F#/E G/E
(Solo)
___ her. An -y girl ___ in the world could have eas - i - ly known me bet-

E5
F#/E G/E 5fr.
D
(Vocal harmony)
(She said,"You're strange,")
A
F#/E G/E F#/E G/E
ter. She said,"You're strange, ___ but don't change,"and I ___

E5
F#/E G/E 5fr.
F#/E G/E F#/E G/E
E5
F#/E G/E 5fr.
F#/E G/E F#/E G/E
(Vocal harmony)
___ let her. ___ 3. In a while, ___

will the smile on my___ face turn to plas - ter, Stick a-

round while the clown who is sick does the trick of dis - as - ter. For the race___

___ of my head_and my face___ is mov-ing much fast - er. Is it strange___

___ I should change? I don't_know, why don't you ask her? Is it strange___

ON THE WAY HOME

When the dream came, I held my breath with my eyes closed.
I went insane, like a smoke ring day when the wind blows.
Now I won't be back till later on,
If I do come back at all.

But you know me, and I miss you now.

In a strange game I saw myself as you knew me,
When the change came, and you had a chance to see through me,
Though the other side is just the same,
You can tell my dream is real,

Because I love you.
Can you sée me now?

Though we rush ahead to save our time,
We are only what we feel,
And I love you,
Can you feel it now?

ON THE WAY HOME

Words and Music by
NEIL YOUNG

Lyrics:

1. When the dream ___ came, I held my breath ___ with my eyes ___ closed. ___ I went in - sane, like a smoke-ring day ___ when the wind ___ blows. ___ Now I won't be back ___ till

2. In a strange ___ game I saw my - self ___ as you knew ___ me, ___ When the change ___ came, and you had a chance ___ to see through ___ me, ___ Though the oth - er side ___ is

C   **F**   **Em7**   **Dm**   *To Coda* ⊕

lat - er on, ___ if I ___ do come ___ back at all. ___
just the same, ___ you can ___ tell my ___ dream is real, ___

G   **Bb**   **F**   **Ebmaj7**   *D.C. al Coda* ⊕

┌─ 3 ─┐   ┌─ 3 ─┐

But you know me, ___ and I miss you now. ___

Coda ⊕   **G**   **Bb**   **F**   **Ebmaj7**

Be-cause I love you. ___ Can you ___ see me ___ now? ___

Fmaj7   **Cmaj7**   **F**   **C**   **Fmaj7**   **Cmaj7**

Though we rush a-head— to save our time,— we are— on-ly— what we feel,— And I love you,— can you— feel it— now?— Yeah.—

WASHINGTON
CALIFORNIA
637 CZK
CULVER CITY DATSU
AVE A HIT WITH THE
UFFALO SPRINGFIELD

I AM A CHILD

I am a child, I last a while.
You can't conceive of the pleasure in my smile.
You hold my hand, rough up my hair,
It's lots of fun to have you there.

I gave to you, now, you give to me,
I'd like to know what you've learned.
The sky is blue and so is the sea.
What is the color, when black is burned
What is the color?

You are a man, you understand.
You pick me up and you lay me down again.
You make the rules, you say what's fair,
It's lots of fun to have you there.

I gave to you, now you give to me,
I'd like to know what you've learned.
The sky is blue and so is the sea.
What is the color, when black is burned
What is the color?

I AM A CHILD

Words and Music by
NEIL YOUNG

Moderately bright Country two-beat

1.-3. I am a child, — *(third time gradual fade to tacet)* I'll last a-while. — You can't con-
2. You are a man, — you un-der-stand. — You pick me up —

ceive of the pleas-ure in my smile. You hold my hand, —
— and you lay — me down a-gain. — You make the rules, —

rough up my hair, —
you say what's fair, — It's lots of fun — to have-you there. —

Dmaj7 5 fr.   **Em7/D** 3 fr.   **D**

God gave to you, ___ now, ___ you give to me, ___

G   **D**   **Dmaj7** 5 fr.

I'd like to know ___ what you've learned. ___ The sky is blue and ___

Em7/D 3 fr.   **D**   **Am7**   **C**

so ___ is the sea. ___ What is ___ the col - or, ___ when black is

Am7   **D**

1.   2. *(To Lyric 3 and fade)*

brown? ___ What is ___ the col - or? ___

L. A.

In a matter of time there'll be a friend of mine, gonna come to the coast
You're gonna see him up close for a minute or two
While the ground cracks under you.
By the look in your eyes you'd think that it was a surprise,
But you seem to forget somethin' somebody said about the bubbles in the sea
And an ocean full of trees and you now.

L. A., uptight, city in the smog, city in the smog.
Don't you wish that you could be here too,
Don't you wish that you could be here too,
Don't you wish that you could be here too?

Well, it's hard to believe, so you get up to leave
And you laugh at the door that you heard it all before.
Oh, it's so good to know that it's all just a show for you.
But when the suppers are planned and the freeways are crammed
And the mountains erupt and the valley is sucked into cracks in the earth,
Will I finally be heard by you?

L.A.

Words and Music by
NEIL YOUNG

Moderately slow

mat-ter of time there'll be a friend of mine, gon-na come to the coast, you're gon-na see him up close for a min-ute or two _ while the

ground cracks un - der you. _

By the look in your eyes _ you'd think that

it was a sur-prise, but you seem to for - get _ some-thin' some-bod-y said _ a-bout the

bub-bles in the sea
and an o - cean
full of trees ___ and you _____ now. ___
L. A., ___
up - tight,
cit - y in the smog,
cit - y in the smog.

Cmaj7
Fmaj7
Don't you wish that you could be here too,
Cmaj7
don't you wish that you could be here too,
Fmaj7
Cmaj7
don't you wish that you could
To Coda
Fmaj7
F
Em
F
be here too?

Well, it's hard to be-lieve, _ so you get up to leave _ and you laugh at the door _ that you heard it all be-fore. Oh, it's so good to know that it's all just a show _ _ for you. _

But when the sup-pers are planned _ and the free-ways are crammed _ and the

moun-tains are rough _ and the val-ley is sucked_ in-to cracks in the earth,

D. S. ⅍ al Coda ⊕

will I fin-al-ly _ be hurt _ by you? _____

Coda
⊕ Fmaj7

THE LAST TRIP TO TULSA

Well I used to drive a cab, you know.
I heard a siren scream,
Pulled over to the corner, and I fell into a dream
There were two men eating pennies and three young girls who cried,
"The West Coast is falling, I see rocks in the sky."
The preacher took his Bible and laid it on the stool,
He said, "With the congregation running, why should I play the fool?"

Well I used to be a woman, you know, I took you for a ride,
I let you fly my airplane, it looked good for your pride,
'Cause you're the kind of man you know, who likes what he says.
I wonder what it's like to be so far over my head.
Well, the lady made the wedding and she brought along the ring,
She got down on her knees, and said, "Let's get on with this thing."

Well, I used to be a folk singer, keeping managers alive,
When you saw me on a corner and told me I was jive.
So I unlocked your mind, you know, to see what I could see,
If you guarantee the postage, I'll mail you back the key.
Well, I woke up in the morning with an arrow through my nose,
There was an Indian in the corner tryin' on my clothes.

Well, I used to be asleep, you know, with blankets on my bed,
I stayed there for a while till they discovered I was dead.
The coroner was friendly, I liked him quite a lot,
If I hadn't've been a woman, I guess I'd never have been caught.
They gave me back my house and car and nothing more was said.

I was drivin' down the freeway when my car ran out of gas
Pulled over to the station, but I was afraid to ask.
The service men were yellow and the gasoline was green,
Although I knew I could not, thought that I was gonna scream.
That was on my last trip to Tulsa, just before the snow,
If you ever need a ride there, be sure to let me know.

I was chopping down a palm tree when a friend dropped by to ask
If I would feel less lonely if he helped me swing the axe.
I said, "No, it's not a case of bein' lonely we have here,
I've been working on this palm tree for eighty seven years."

I said, "No, it's not a case of being lonely we have here,
I've been workin' on this palm tree for eighty seven years."
He said, "Go get lost," and walked t'ward his Cadillac,
I chopped down the palm tree and it landed on his back.

THE LAST TRIP TO TULSA

Words and Music by
NEIL YOUNG

Slowly

A(add2)

A(add2)

Play three times

p

1. Well I used _ to drive _ a cab, you know. _

C

D

I heard a si - ren scream, _

Pulled o - ver to the cor - ner, _

C

A(add2)

and I fell _ in - to a dream. _

There were

C

two men eat - ing pen - nies _

and three _ young girls _ who cried, _

"The West Coast is fall-ing, I see rocks in the sky." The

preach-er took his Bi - ble and laid it on the stool, He said, "With the

con-gre-ga-tion run - ning, why should I play the fool?"

Play three times

2. Well I used to be a wom-an, you know, I took you for a ride,

I let you fly my air-plane, it looked good for your pride, ___ 'Cause you're_

_ the kind_of man_you know, who likes what he says. ___ I won-der what it's like to be so far_

o - ver my head." ____ Well, the la-dy made _ the wed-ding _ and she

brought a-long the ring, _ She got down on_ her knees,_ and said, "Let's get on_ with this thing." _

A tempo

3. Well, I used to be a folk singer,

Play three times

mf

keep-ing man-ag-ers a - live, _____ When you saw me on a cor - ner and

told me I ____ was jive. _____ So I

un-locked your mind, _ you know, to see _ what I _ could see, _ If you guar-an-tee the post-age, _ I'll mail you back the key. Well, I

woke up in the morn - ing with an ar - row through my nose, There was an

In - di - an in the cor - ner try - in' on my clothes.

Play four times   *Play five times*

A tempo

4. Well, I used to be a - sleep, you know, with blan - kets on my bed,

I stayed there for a while ____ till they dis-cov-ered I _ was dead. _

The cor-o-ner was _ friend-ly, _ I liked him _ quite a lot, _

If I had-n't-'ve been a wom-an, I guess I'd nev-er have been caught.

They gave me back ____ my house _ and car _ and noth-ing more _ was said.

A tempo

Play ten times

mf (Double-time feeling)

5. I was driv - in' down the Free - way _ when my _

_ car _ ran out of _ gas _ Pulled o - ver to _ the sta - tion, _ but I

was a - fraid _ to ask. _ The

serv - ice men _ were yel - low _ and the gas - o - line _ was green, _ al-though_ I knew_ I could not, thought that I _____ was gon-na scream. _

That was on my last_ trip_ to Tul-sa, _ just be-fore_ the snow, _____ If you

ev-er need a ride_ there, be sure_ to let me know. _

Play several times

Rubato

6. I was chop-ping down_ a palm_tree when a friend_dropped by to ask _____

If I would feel ____ less lone - ly if he helped me swing __ the axe. __

I said, "No, ___ it's not a case __ of be - in' lone -ly

we have here, _____ I've been work -ing on this __ palm tree __ for

eight - y-sev -en years." __

Play several times

A(add2)　　　　　　　　　　　　　　　　C

7. I said,　"No, __ it's not a case of be-ing　lone-ly we have here, __

D　　　　　　　　　　　　　　　　C　　A7

Tacet

I've been work-in' on this palm _ tree　for　eight - y - sev - en years." ____

E

He said,　"Go get　lost," _ and walked t'ward _ his　Ca-dil -lac, _____

D　　　　　　　D(sus4)　　　C

I chopped down the palm _ tree　and ___ it land-ed　on　his　back.

THE LONER

He's a perfect stranger like a cross of himself and a fox.
He's a feeling arranger and a changer of the ways he talks.
He's the unforeseen danger the keeper of the key to the locks.
Know when you see him, nothing can free him.
Step aside, open wide, it's the loner.

If you see him in the subway, he'll be down at the end of the car,
Watching you move until he knows he knows who you are.
When you get off at your station alone, he'll know that you are.
Know when you see him, nothing can free him.
Step aside, open wide, it's the loner.

There was a woman he knew about a year or so ago.
She had something that he needed and he pleaded with her not to go.
On the day that she left, he died—but it did not show.
Know when you see him, nothing can free him.
Step aside, open wide, it's the loner.

THE LONER

Words and Music by
NEIL YOUNG

Moderate Rock

1. He's the per-fect stran-ger like a cross of him-self and a fox.

He's a feel-ing ar-rang-er and a chang-er of the ways he talks. He's the

* Guitarist: Tune first and sixth strings to D (D A D G B D)

un-fore-seen dan-ger and the keep-er of the key___ to the locks.___

Know___ when you see him,___ noth - ing can

free him.___ Step___ a-side, o - pen wide,_____ it's the lon - er.

(Percussion)

2. If you

see him in the sub-way, he'll be down— at the end of the car,—

Watch-ing you move— un-til he knows,— he knows— who you are.—

When you get off at your sta-tion a-lone,—

———— he'll know— that you are.—

Know_ when you see him,_____ noth - ing can free him.___

Step_ a-side, o - pen wide,_____ it's the lon - er.___

To Coda ⊕

(Percussion)

mp

3. There was a

wom-an he knew_ a-bout a year_ or so_ a - go.___

f

She had some-thing that he need-ed and he plead-ed with her not to go.

On the day that she left, he died but it did not show.

D.S. % al Coda ⊕

Repeat and fade

Coda ⊕

mp Repeat and fade

IF I COULD HAVE HER TONIGHT

All of a sudden she was on my mind,
I wasn't ready for her kind,
And she was takin' her time

Oh if she came to me, would she be kind?
And if she stayed with me, do you think that she'd like to do
Anything I would, or would she leave me?

If I could have her tonight. Does she want to go?
Look at those eyes. Does she want to?
If I could have her tonight.
If I could have her tonight, if I could have her tonight.

Lately I've found myself losing my mind,
Knowing how badly I need her,
It's something hard to find.

IF I COULD HAVE HER TONIGHT

Words and Music by
NEIL YOUNG

Moderately

D5(add2)   D

1. All of a sud-den she was on
2. Late-ly I've found my-self

D6   Dmaj7   G

on my mind, _ I was-n't read-y for her ____ kind, ____
los-ing my mind, _ Know-ing how bad-ly I need ____ her, ____

Em   B♭   Em

and she was tak-in' her time. _
it's some-thing hard to find. _

But, ___ if she came ___ to me, ___
would she be kind? ___ And ___ if she stayed ___ with me, ___ do you
think that she'd like ___ to do an - y - thing I ___ would, or would she leave ___ me? ___
If I could have her to - night. ___ Does she want to go? ___ Look at those eyes. ___

(Vocal harmony)

D7

(Unison)

Does she want to? If I could have her to-night,_

G

D

_ if I could have her to-night,_ if I could have her to-night._

D6

Dmaj7

G

Em

gradual fade

Gm7

Em7♭5

A

A7

C

(pp) *continue fade*

pppp - *to tacet*

I'VE BEEN WAITING FOR YOU

I've been looking for a woman to save my life,
Not to beg or borrow,
A woman with the feeling of losing once or twice.
Who knows how it could be tomorrow?

I've been waiting for you, and you've been coming to me
For such a long time now, such a long time now.

I'VE BEEN WAITING FOR YOU

Words and Music by
NEIL YOUNG

Moderately

I've been look-ing _____ for a wom-an to save my_ life, Not _ to beg or to bor - row, _____ A wom-an _ with the feel-ing _ of los - ing once or twice.___ Who knows_how it could be _ to - mor - row.

I've been wait-ing for you, _ and you've_been com-ing- to me ___

For such a long_time now, such a long_time now, ___

1. I've been
2. such a

Repeat and fade

long_time now, such a long time_ now, ___ Such a

Repeat and fade

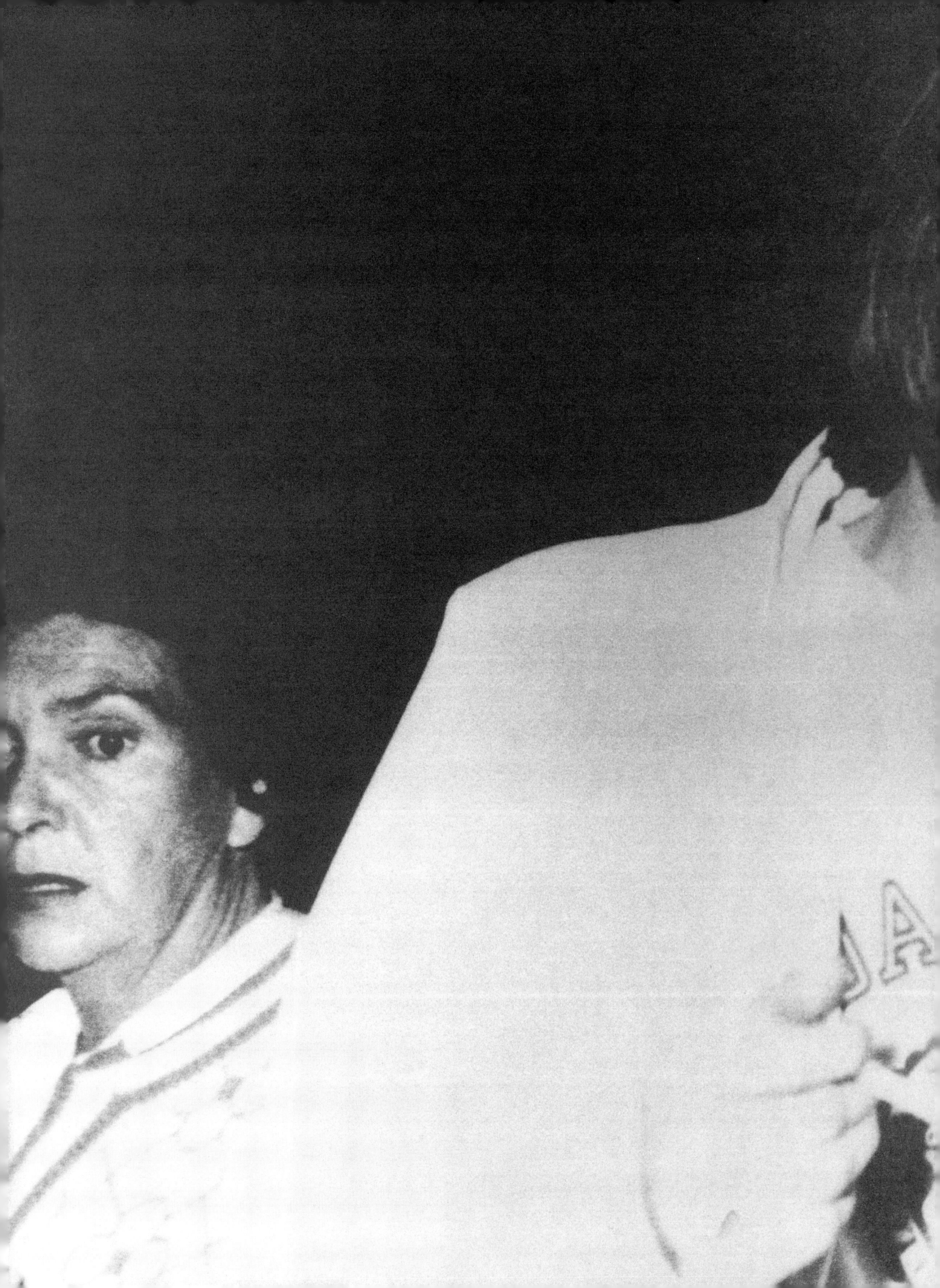

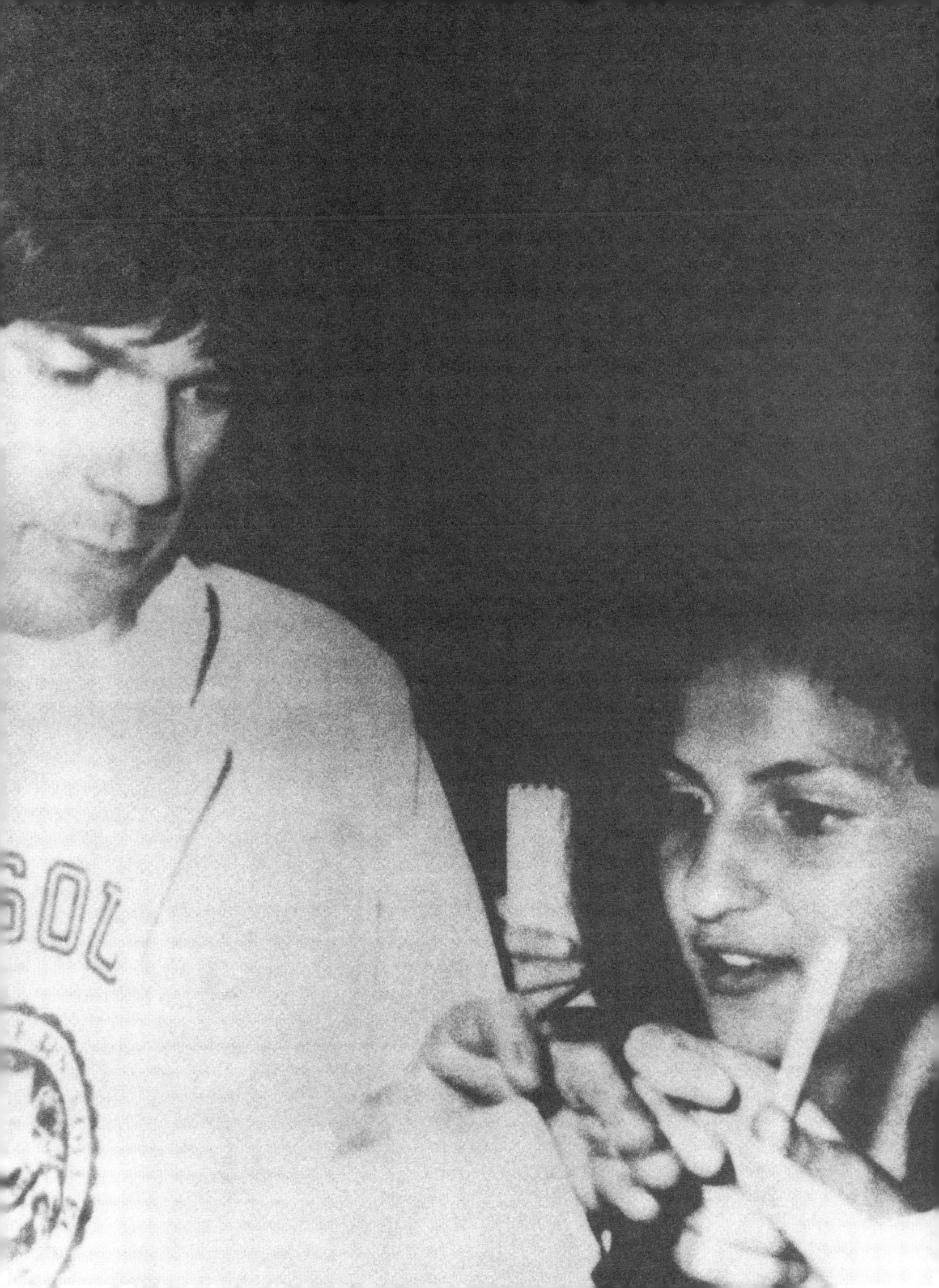

HERE WE ARE IN THE YEARS

Now that the holidays have come,
They can relax and watch the sun rise above
All of the beautiful things they've done.

Go to the country, take the dog,
Look at the sky without the smog,
See the world, laugh at the farmers feeding hogs, eat hot dogs.

What a pity that the people from the city
Can't relate to the slower things
That the country brings.

Time itself is bought and sold,
The spreading fear of growing old
Contains a thousand foolish games that we play.
While people planning trips to stars
Allow another boulevard to claim a quiet country lane,
It's insane

So the subtle face is a loser this time around.
Here we are in the years where the showman shifts the gears,
Lives become careers, children cry in fear, "Let us out of here!"

HERE WE ARE IN THE YEARS

Words and Music by
NEIL YOUNG

Now that the hol - i - days_ have
Go to the coun - try, take_ the dog,_

come, they can re-lax_ and watch_ the sun_ rise a - bove_ all of the beau-
look at the sky_ with-out_ the smog,_ see the world,_ laugh at the farm-

ti - ful things they've done.
ers feed - ing hogs,

eat hot

dogs. What a pit - y that the peo - ple from the

cit - y can't re - late___ to the slow - er things___ that the

coun - try brings.___

(Solo)

Time it - self is bought and sold, the

Em
Bm
Bm7
C
(Vocal harmony)
spread-ing fear of grow-ing old con-tains a thou-sand fool-ish games that we
G
Gsus4
G
Gsus4
G
(Solo)
Gsus4
G
play. While peo-ple plan-ning trips to stars al-
Em
Bm
Bm7
C
(Vocal harmony)
low an-oth-er boul-e-vard to claim a qui-et coun-try lane, it's in-
G
Gsus4
G
A
Asus4
A
G
D
Bm7
E5
sane.

Em7 **Dmaj7** **Em7** **Dmaj7**

(Solo)

mp

So the sub-tle face_____ is a los-er this time__ a-round.__

G **A** **D**

(Vocal harmony)

mf

Here we are__ in the years__ where the show-man shifts__ the gears,

marcato

G **D** **G** **A**

Brighter tempo ($\frac{9}{8}$ feeling)

lives be-come__ ca-reers, chil-dren cry__ in fear, "Let us out__ of here!"_____

Asus4 **Em7** **Asus4** **A** **Asus4** **F#**

Very slowly

F **D** **A**

Repeat and fade

gradual ritard.

(Sound of footsteps)

Repeat and fade

(Let ring)

THE OLD LAUGHING LADY

Don't call pretty Peggy, she can't hear you no more.
Don't leave no message 'round her back door.
They say the Old Laughing Lady been here before.
She don't keep time, she don't count score.

You can't have a cupboard if there ain't no wall.
You got to move. There's no time left to stall.
They say the Old Laughing Lady dropped by to call.
When she leaves, she leaves nothing at all.

See the drunkard of the village falling on the street.
Can't tell his ankles from the rest of his feet.
He loves his old laughing lady 'cause her taste is so sweet.
But the laughing lady's lovin', ain't the kind he can keep.

There's a fever on the freeway, blacks out the night.
There's a slipping on the stairway, just don't feel right.
And there's a rumbling in the bedroom and a flashing of light.
There's the Old Laughing Lady, ev'rything is all right.

THE OLD LAUGHING LADY

Words and Music by
NEIL YOUNG

1. Don't call pret-ty Peg - gy,

she can't hear you no more. Don't leave no mes-sage

'round her back door. They say the

* **Guitarists: Tune strings to D A D G B D**

"Old_ Laugh-ing La - dy"_____ been here_ be-fore._

She don't keep time,_____ she don't count_ score._

(Percussion)

2. You can't_ have a cup - board_ if there ain't_ no_ wall._

You got to move,____

There's no time left to stall.____ They say the

"Old Laugh-ing La - dy"____ dropped by to call.____ (Strings)

When she leaves,____ she leaves noth-ing__ at all.____

(Percussion)

Dmaj7 Dm7 Dmaj7 Dm7 G/D Dmaj7 Dm7 Dmaj7 Dm7 G/D D
6 fr. 5 fr. 6 fr. 5 fr. 7 fr. 6 fr. 5 fr. 6 fr. 5 fr. 7 fr.
mf
subito mp
D
Em/D
4 fr.
3. See the drunk-ard of the vil - lage___ fall - ing___ on the street,_
fe - ver on the free - way,___ blacks out the
Dmaj7
6 fr.
Em/D
4 fr.
D
night._ Can't tell his an - kles
There's a slip-ping___ on the stair - way,
Em/D
4 fr.
Dmaj7
6 fr.
G/D
7 fr.
from the rest_ of his feet.___
just don't__ feel right.___
He loves his old_
And there's a rum-

G `3 fr.`

laugh-ing la - dy _____ 'cause her taste_____ is so_____ sweet._____
bling in the bed - room_____ and a flash - ing of light._____

D

Em/D `4 fr.`   **Dmaj7** `6 fr.`   *To Coda* ⊕   **Dm7** `5 fr.`   **G** `3 fr.`

But the laugh-ing la-dy's lov-in',_____ ⎫
There's the "Old___ Laughing La - dy",___ ⎭ ain't the kind___ he can keep._____

(Percussion)

D   ***D/B♭***   **D/C**   **D**

D.S. 𝄋 *al Coda* ⊕

4. There's a

mf   *subito* **mp**

Repeat and fade

Dm7 `5 fr.`   **C(addD)**   **C(addD)**

Coda ⊕

ev-'ry-thing_ is all right._____

Repeat and fade

* **Play D/B♭ instead of D on repeat**

WHAT DID YOU DO TO MY LIFE?

When we were living together, I thought that I knew you would stay,
Still when you left me, I tried to pretend we could make it some way.

I don't care if all of the mountains turn to dust in the air,
(What did you do to my life?)
It isn't fair that I should wake up at dawn and not find you there.
What did you do to my life?

It's hard enough losing without the confusion of knowing I tried,
But you've made your mind up that I'll be alone now,
There's nothing to hide.

WHAT DID YOU DO TO MY LIFE?

Words and Music by
NEIL YOUNG

Moderately

When we were liv - ing to - geth-er, I thought that I knew you would stay,
hard e-nough los - ing with - out the con-fu - sion of know-ing I tried,

still when you left — me, I tried to pre-tend — we could
but you've made your mind — up that I'll be a - lone, — now there's

make it some way. ———
noth-ing to hide. ———

I don't care — if

all of the moun-tains turn to dust in the air,_ (What did you do_ to my

It is-n't fair_ that I should wake up_ at dawn and not find you there._
life?_____)

What did you do_ to my life?_____

It's _

EVERYBODY KNOWS THIS IS NOWHERE

I think I'd like to go back home and take it easy
There's a woman that I'd like to get to know livin' there.
Everybody seems to wonder what it's like down here.

I gotta get away from this day-to-day runnin' around,
Everybody knows this is nowhere.
Everybody, everybody knows, everybody knows this is nowhere.

Every time I think about back home, it's cool and breezy.
I wish that I could be there right now, just passing time.
Everybody seems to wonder what it's like down here.

I gotta get away from this day-to-day runnin' around,
Everybody knows this is nowhere.
Everybody, everybody knows, everybody knows this is nowhere.

BY NEIL YOUNG © 1969 COTILLION MUSIC, INC. and BROKEN FIDDLE
All rights administered by WARNER-TAMERLANE PUBLISHING CORP.
All Rights Reserved

EVERYBODY KNOWS THIS IS NOWHERE

Words and Music by
NEIL YOUNG

Moderate double-time country feeling

1. I think I'd like to go — back home — and take it eas - y, There's a wom - an that I'd like to get to know — a-liv-in' there.

Ev - 'ry-bod-y seems to won - der — what it's like down here. — I got-ta get a-way from this day-to-day run-nin' a - round,__ Ev-'ry-bod-y knows this is no-

where.

Ev-'ry-bod-y, ev-'ry-bod-y knows,_____ ev-'ry-bod-y

knows this_ is no - where.

2. Ev-'ry time I think a-bout back home,__ it's cool and breez - y.

I

D.S. % al Coda
C G C G C G
wish that I could be _ there right now, _ just pass-ing time.
Coda
C G C
Ev-'ry-bod-y knows, ______ ev-'ry-bod-y knows, _ ev-'ry-bod-y
G C G
knows, _ ev-'ry-bod-y, ev-'ry-bod-y knows _ this is no-where. Ev-'ry bod-y knows, _ ev-'ry bod-y
Repeat and fade
C G C
knows. _
Repeat and fade

CINNAMON GIRL

I want to live with a Cinnamon Girl,
I could be happy the rest of my life with a Cinnamon Girl.
A dreamer of pictures, I run in the night
You see us together, chasin' the moonlight, my Cinnamon Girl.

Ten silver saxes, a bass with a bow,
The drummer relaxes and waits between shows for his Cinnamon Girl.
A dreamer of pictures, I run in the night
You see us together, chasin' the moonlight, my Cinnamon Girl.

Ma send me money now, I'm gonna make it somehow
I need another chance.
You see your baby loves to dance, yeah, yeah, yeah.

CINNAMON GIRL

Words and Music by
NEIL YOUNG

Moderately

(Vocal harmony)

I wan-na live with a

Cin-na-mon Girl,___ I can be hap-py the rest of my life___ with a

* Guitarists: Tune first and sixth strings to D (D A D G B D)

Cin - na - mon Girl.___ A dream-er of pic - tures, I

run in the night,___ you see us to - geth - er, chas-in' the moon - light, my

Cin - na - mon Girl.___

Ten sil - ver sax - es, a bass with a bow, __ the drum-mer re - lax - es and

waits be - tween shows __ for the Cin - na - mon Girl. __

dream - er of pic - tures, I run in the night, __ you see us to - geth - er,

chas - in' the moon - light, my Cin - na - mon Girl. __

C/D D C G/B A F G C/D D C G/B A F
5 fr. 7 fr. 5 fr. 5 fr. 7 fr.
Csus2
Pa sent me mon - ey, now I'm gon - na make it some - how, I need an - oth - er chance.
Gm7
3 fr.
Am7sus4
you see your ba - by loves to dance, yeah, yeah,
A7sus4
F G D/A Am7 sus4 D/A C G/B C Am7 sus4 C/D D
5 fr. 5 fr. 7 fr. 5 fr. 7 fr.
yeah.

RUNNING DRY
(Requiem For The Rockets)

Oh, please help me, oh please help me, I'm livin' by myself.
I need someone to comfort me, I need someone to tell.

I'm sorry for the things I've done,
I've shamed myself with lies,
But soon these things are overcome and can't be recognized.

I left my love with ribbons on and water in her eyes.
I took from her the love I'd won and turned it to the sky.

I'm sorry for the things I've done,
I've shamed myself with lies,
My cruelty has punctured me and now I'm running dry.

RUNNING DRY
(Requiem For The Rockets)

Words and Music by
NEIL YOUNG

Lyrics:

Oh, please help me, oh, please help me, I'm liv-in' by my-self.
I need some-one to com-fort me, I need some-one to tell.

left my love with rib-bons on and wa-ter in her eyes.
I took from her the love I'd won and turned it to the sky.

I'm
I'm

sor - ry for the things I've done, I've shamed my - self with
sor - ry for the things I've done, I've shamed my - self with

lies, but soon these things are o - ver - come and
lies, my cru - el - ty has punc - tured - me and

To Coda ⊕

can't be— re - cog — nized.
now I'm— run - ning— dry.

1. | 2. *D.S.* 𝄋 *al Coda* ⊕

I   I'm

Coda ⊕

nized.

Repeat and fade

(When You're On) THE LOSING END

I went into town to see you yesterday but you were not home.
So I talked to some old friends for a while before I wandered off alone.

It's so hard for me now but I'll make it somehow,
Though I know I'll never be the same.
Won't you ever change your ways,
It's so hard to make love pay when you're on the losing end,
And I feel that way again.

Well, I miss you more than ever,
Since you've gone I can hardly maintain.
Things are different round here ev'ry night, my tears fall down like rain.

It's so hard for me now but I'll make it somehow,
Though I know I'll never be the same.
Won't you ever change your ways,
It's so hard to make love pay when you're on the losing end.
And I feel that way again.

(When You're On) THE LOSING END

Words and Music by
NEIL YOUNG

Moderately

I went in -

to town — to see — you yes-ter-day — but you were — not —
— you more than ev - er, since you've gone — I can hard-ly main -

home.—
tain. —

So I talked —
Things are

to some old friends for a-while before I wan-dered off
dif-f'rent round here ev-'ry night, my tears fall down

a - lone.
like rain.

(Vocal harmony)

It's so

hard for me now but I'll make it some-how, though I

know I'll nev-er be the same. Won't you ev-er change your ways, it's so hard to make love pay when you're on the los - ing end,

and I'll feel that way a - gain.

Well, I miss

COWGIRL IN THE SAND

Hello, Cowgirl in the sand.
Is this place at your command?
Can I stay here for a while?
Can I see your sweet, sweet smile?

Old enough, now, to change your name.
When so many love you, is it the same?
It's the woman in you that makes you want to play this game.

Hello, ruby in the dust.
Has your band begun to rust?
After all the sin we've had,
I was hoping that we'd turn bad.

(Chorus)

Hello, woman of my dreams.
Is this not the way it seems?
Purple words on a gray background
To be a woman and to be turned down.

(Chorus)

COWGIRL IN THE SAND

Words and Music by
NEIL YOUNG

Slowly, double time feeling

Play several times

(L.H. optional 8va bassa throughout)

mf

1. Hel-lo, Cow - girl_ in the

sand.

(Vocal answer)

(Hel-lo Cow-girl in the sand.)_____ Is this place_ at_ your com - mand?_____

Can I stay here for a_ while? _____ Can I see your sweet,_ sweet smile?

Old e - nough,_ now, to change your name._ When so man - y love_ you, is it the same?__ It's the wom-an in you that makes you want to play this game._____

Play several times

(on D.S.)

(Vocal answers)

2. Hel-lo, ru-by in the dust.__ Has your band__ be-gun to rust?__
3. Hel-lo, wom-an of my dreams.__ Is this not __ the way it seems?__

2. (Hel-lo, ru-by in the dust.___)
3. (Hel-lo, wom-an of my dreams.__)

Af - ter all the sin__ we've had,__ I was hop -ing that
Pur-ple words on a gray back - ground__ to be a wom-an and to

Fmaj7　　G　　Dm　　Em　　C　F　　Dm　　Em

we'd_turn back.
be__turned down,　Old e - nough,_now, to change your name._ When so man-y love_ you, is

C　F　(Vocal harmony)　Dm　C　F

it the same?_ It's the wom-an in you that makes you want to play this game._____

C　(♪=♪)　E7　A　　To Coda⊕　　D.S. ％ al Coda⊕

Coda⊕　E7　A　Repeat and fade　Am　F

Repeat and fade

DOWN BY THE RIVER

Be on my side, I'll be on your side, baby.
There is no reason for you to hide.
It's so hard for me stayin' here all alone
When you could be takin' me for a ride.

She could drag me over the rainbow and send me away.
Down by the river, I shot my baby.
Down by the river, dead, ooh, shot her dead.

You take my hand, I'll take your hand,
Together we may get away
This much madness is too much sorrow,
It's impossible to make it today.

(Chorus)

DOWN BY THE RIVER

Words and Music by
NEIL YOUNG

Moderately slow

Be on my_ side, I'll be on your_ side,_ ba - by, there is no rea - son for

you to hide. _____ It's so hard for me stay-in'_ here all a - lone _____ when you could be tak-in' me — for a ride, _____ yeah,

yeah. _____ She could drag me o-ver the rain-bow ____

and send me a-way. _____ Down by the __

riv - er, I shot my _ ba - by.

Down by the — riv - er, dead,

ooh, _____ shot her dead. _____

You take my hand, I'll take your hand,_ to-geth-er we may_ get away. _____

This much mad — ness _ is _____ too much sor - row, _

it's im - pos - si - ble _ to make it _ to - day, _____ yeah, _____ ooh,

ooh, yeah. _____ She could drag me o - ver the rain - bow _____

and send me a - way. _____ Down by the _ riv - er,

gradual cresc.

I shot my_ ba - by.   Down by the _ riv - er,

dead, ____   dead, _ woh, ___ woh, _ shot her dead,   shot her dead. ___

mp

D.S. % al Coda ⊕

mp

Coda
⊕

Repeat and fade

riv - er.   Down by the _ riv - er,   I shot my_ ba - by.

Repeat and fade

ROUND AND ROUND AND ROUND

Round and round and round we spin,
To weave a wall to hem us in,
It won't be long, it won't be long
How slow and slow and slow it goes,
To mend the tear that always shows.
It won't be long, it won't be long.

It's hard enough losin' the paper illusion you've hidden inside,
Without the confusion of findin' you're usin' the crutch of the lie
To shelter your pride when you cry.

Chorus

Now you're movin' too slow and wherever you go there's another beside.
It's so hard to say no to yourself and it shows that you're losing inside,
When you step on your pride and you cry.

Chorus

How the hours will bend through the time that you spend till you turn to your eyes,
And you see your best friend looking over the end and you turn to see why,
And he looks in your eyes and he cries.

ROUND AND ROUND AND ROUND

Words and Music by
NEIL YOUNG

Moderately, with 9/8 feeling

1.,2.,3.,4. Round and round and round we spin, to weave a wall to hem us in, It won't be long,_____ it won't be long._____

How slow and slow and slow it

goes, to mend the tear that al - ways shows. It

won't be long,_____ it won't be

Fourth time to Coda ⊕

long._____

1.   It's
2. Now   you're
3. How   the

G

hard e-nough los-in' the pa - per il - lu - sion you've
groov - in' too slow and wher - ev - er you go there's an -
hours____ will bend through the time that you spend till you

Am   **D**   **G**

hid -den in - side,____ With - out the con -
oth - er be - sides.____ It's so hard to say
turn to your eyes,____ And you see your best

Am

fu - sion of find - in' you're us - in' the crutch of the
no to your-self and it shows that you're los - ing in -
friend look - ing o - ver the end and you turn to see

D   **Cm**

lie____
side,____
why,____ When you step on your____ pride____
And he looks in your____ eyes____
To shel - ter your____ pride____

when you cry._____
and you cry._____
and he

cries._____

Coda

Repeat and fade
(Vocal harmony)

D.S. %
al Coda

Ooh,_____
Ooh,_____
ooh,_____

Repeat and fade
R.H.

ooh,_____
ooh,_____
Ooh,_____

DANCE DANCE DANCE

Never thought love had a rainbow on it,
Used to think a cloud was a nightmare,
That was up until when I first met you,
Now I go around hoping you care.

Dance, dance, feel it all around you, dance, dance, dance.
Never thought love had a rainbow on it, see the girl dance,
See the girl dance.

Mississippi mud never touched her fingers,
California sand lies in her hand,
Love her more than life as the daylight lingers,
Early in the morning I'll be her man.

Dance, dance, feel it all around you, dance, dance, dance.
Mississippi mud never touched her fingers, see the girl dance,
See the girl dance.

DANCE DANCE DANCE

Words and Music by
NEIL YOUNG

Moderately

Nev-er thought love had a rain-bow on it, used to think a cloud was a night-mare,
Mis-sis-sip-pi mud nev-er touched her fin-gers, Cal-i-for-nia sand lies in her hand,

that was up un-til when I first met you, now I go a-round hop-ing you care.
love her more than life as the day-light lin-gers, ear-ly in the morn-ing I'll be her man.

Dance, dance, feel it all a-round you, dance, dance, dance.
Dance, dance, feel it all a-round you, dance, dance, dance.

Nev-er thought love had a rain-bow on it, see the girl_ dance,
Mis-sis-sip-pi mud nev-er touched her fin-gers, see the girl_ dance,

see the girl_ dance.
see the girl_ dance.

Dance, dance, feel it all a-round you dance, dance, dance.

Mis-sis-sip-pi mud nev-er touched her fin-gers, see the girl_ dance,

see the girl_dance, see the girl_dance.

WONDERIN'

I been walkin' all night long,
My footsteps made me crazy,
Baby, you been gone too long,

I'm wonderin' if you'll come home,
I'm hopin' that you'll be my lady.
I'm wonderin' if I'll be alone,
Knowin' that I need you to save me.

I've been workin' all day long
To keep my heart from sadness,
But, Baby, you been away too long,

I'm wonderin' if you'll come home,
I'm hopin' that you'll be my lady.
I'm wonderin' if I'll be alone,
Knowin' that I need you to save me.
I'm wonderin', I'm wonderin', I'm wonderin',

WONDERIN'

Words and Music by
NEIL YOUNG

Moderately

Lyrics:
I been walk-in' all night long,__ my foot-steps made me cra-zy, Ba-by, you been gone__ too long,__ I'm won-der-in' if you'll come home,__ I'm hop-in' that you'll__ be my la - dy. I'm

F C/D G F
won-der-in' if I'll be a-lone, know-in' that I need you to save
C C/D G C G D G C
me.
R.H.
G D G C/E D G
I've been work-in' all day long to keep my heart from sad-ness,
Bm Am7 G F
but, Ba-by, you been a-way too long, I'm won-der-in' if

you'll come home, _ I'm hop-in' that you'll _ be my la - dy. I'm

won-der-in' if I'll be a - lone, _ Know-in' that I need you to save _

— me. I'm won-der-in', I'm won-der-in', _____

I'm won-der-in', _ I'm won-der-in'. _____